UPLIFT

12 Weeks to a Happier & Brighter YOU...

UPLIFT

12 Weeks to a Happier & Brighter YOU...

Dr. Vrushali Saraswat

Worldwide Published by
Pendown Press
PREMIUM BUSINESS PUBLISHER

PENDOWN PRESS LLP

An ISO 9001 & ISO 14001 Certified Co.,
Regd. Office: 3767A, Kanhaiya Nagar,
Tri Nagar, Delhi-110035
Ph.: 8130886000, 9650072927
E-mail: info@pendownpress.com
Branch Office: 1A/2A, 20, Hari Sadan, Ansari Road,
Daryaganj, New Delhi-110002
Ph.: 011-45794768
Website: PendownPress.com

Edition: 2025

ISBN: 978-93-6338-476-7

Layout and Cover Designed by Pendown Graphics Team
Printed and Bound in India by Thomson Press India Ltd.

Dedication to...

Amit, my life partner
and unwavering pillar,
and
Asmi and Atharva,
my beautiful children,
You are my compass and my courage

CONTENTS

ACKNOWLEDGEMENTS

From the heart of Dr. Vrushali Saraswat

This book, like every meaningful endeavour in life, is not the work of one person alone. It takes a village, and I have been blessed with mine.

Gratitude to all my teachers and mentors, thank you. Your wisdom, patience, and belief have shaped the woman I am today. A special note of gratitude to Dr. Newton Kondawati and Dr. Laxmi Kondawati, your teachings are etched into my spirit and have become the foundation of my personal and professional values.

Grateful to Dr. Rahul Malushte and Dr. Jayesh Shah, thank you for introducing me to QLU and opening new doors for me.

I am grateful to my Late grandmother, the Late Mrs Gulabbai Joshi, who instilled self-respect and responsibility consciousness in me. I have imbibed her boldness and ambition.

To my parents, Dr. C.M. Joshi and Mrs. Sarita Joshi, you've built me from the ground up. Your values, love, and discipline continue to be my inner strength.

Dr. Ajit Kulkarni, Sir, your teachings did not just enhance my understanding of the human mind; they nurtured my soul. Receiving a foreword from you and Dr. Newton feels nothing short of a divine blessing. Words will always fall short of the gratitude I hold in my heart for both of you.

Heartfelt gratitude to Mr. Ankur Warikoo, Smt Rajeshwari Modi (RajDidi), Mr. Shyam Pathak, and Dr. C.H. Asrani, who have read the manuscript and given their endorsement, giving me immense courage and motivation to go forward in the work which I believe in wholeheartedly.

To my incredible team, Sneha, Mayuri, Shubhangi, and Swarali, thank you for standing beside me, building HHC's vision, and holding the fort in ways I can't always put into words. I lean on you more than you know.

To Rahul Jain Sir, thank you for stretching the boundaries of my vision, and to Akshar Yadav Sir, your guidance has given wings to my dreams.

To Swarali Yadav, thank you for designing the cover page so thoughtfully. Your work reflects the essence of this journey.

To my dearest Asmi and Atharva, thank you for being my constant. Just your presence gives my life renewed meaning and purpose. Being your mother has changed me deeply. The way you've supported me, especially during chaotic schedules and long working hours with so much love, grace, and maturity, humbles me. You are my honest critics, my biggest cheerleaders, and my deepest joy.

And to Amit, this book wouldn't exist without you. You don't just support my dreams, you live them with me. Even when I falter, you see the best in me. At my lowest, you've always stood tall for both of us. Thank you for being my strength, my mirror, and my home.

To the late Mr. B.R. Saraswat, my father-in-law, your legacy continues to guide me. This book is a tribute to the values you stood for. To Mrs Nisha Saraswat, my mother-in-law, and Arati Sharma, my sister-in-law, your wisdom and quiet strength are priceless gifts in my life.

And to my maiden family, Vaibhav, Megha, Ishita, Vikram, and Supriya, your love lifts me, always encouraging me to aim higher.

Heartfelt gratitude to Dinesh Verma, CEO of Pendown Press, and their editing team for putting up with the creative whims that I have shown in our journey together and delivering smoothly.

Lastly, I am grateful to all the patients and my huge friend circle, who have genuinely taught me these life lessons, which I present in front of you.

From the depths of my being, thank you. Each of you has left your imprint on these pages.

Thank you, thank you, thank you!

"I am a ripple in a sacred stream of blessings, carried by love, carved by faith, and lit by the quiet light of those who walked with me, even in spirit."

Dr. Vrushali Saraswat

❖ ❖ ❖

PREFACE

There was once a little girl who never walked; she only ran, hopped, skipped, and flew. It felt as if the wind had made a home under her feet. Life was light. Effortless.

But somewhere between growing up and growing older, the wind stopped showing up.

One day, even walking felt heavy. Smiling became a task. And laughter... a forgotten luxury.

This wasn't just her story, it was the story of so many. I remember hearing it from a patient of mine who had achieved so much in life, yet said these words with such honesty that it struck something deep within me.

I realised growing up doesn't have to mean growing out of joy. But sadly, that's exactly what happens to most of us. We move from wonder to worry, from curiosity to calculation.

Over the last 25 years of practice, I've sat across thousands of people each with their own journeys, each struggling to maintain the delicate balance of the mind. And the one missing piece I found again and again was Happiness.

That's where Uplift was born.

Not as a quick fix or a perfect path.

But as a heartfelt compilation of the tools, methods, and little rituals I've seen work again and again to help people come back to themselves.

Because I truly believe that happiness isn't a luxury. It's our right. And no one should have to fight alone to feel alive again.

With deep gratitude in my heart, I offer this to you not as a guidebook, but as a companion. A soft nudge toward lightness.

And a heartfelt invitation to rediscover your wings.

Yours in joy

Dr. Vrushali Saraswat

❖ ❖ ❖

Foreword Dr. Newton

In the intricate tapestry of human existence, we find ourselves uniquely capable of questioning our experiences and the very nature of reality. Unlike the animal kingdom, where survival instincts reign supreme, humans possess an extraordinary drive to seek joy and alleviate suffering. While we may occasionally succumb to fear and aggression—instincts reminiscent of our animal counterparts—there lies within us a profound impetus to rise above mere survival. This journey toward higher consciousness invites us to explore the depths of our thoughts, beliefs, and emotions, recognizing their pivotal role in shaping the experiences we create in our lives.

As research has shown, the complexity of human nature necessitates an awakening from the slumber of unawareness. It is through this awakening that we can begin to master our minds, reframe limiting beliefs, and transform our emotional landscapes. Many have embarked on this transformative journey, dedicating themselves to persistent practice and effort, ultimately discovering the possibility of enhancing the quality of their lives.

In this spirit of growth and enlightenment, we are fortunate to have Dr. Vrushali Saraswat—a holistic happiness coach and healer—who has dedicated her life to guiding others on this path. Her book, Uplift: 12 Weeks to a Happier, Brighter You, offers readers accessible and practical tools to facilitate profound change. Through her insights and compassionate approach, Dr. Saraswat invites us to embrace our potential for transformation, encouraging us to take meaningful steps towards discovering our best selves.

I wholeheartedly encourage everyone to approach this book with curiosity and openness. The wisdom contained within its pages has the power to uplift and inspire, fostering a journey of self-discovery that can lead to a more fulfilling and joyful existence. My sincere best wishes go to Dr. Vrushali Saraswat for her unwavering commitment to making a difference in the lives of many.

With love and light,

Dr. Newton Kondaveti,

MBBS & MD

Founder & Chairman of QLU
(Proposed Quantum Life University)

www.qluglobal.org

❖ ❖ ❖

FOREWORD DR. AJIT

"Uplift" - a title as graceful as its essence - emerges as a luminous offering from Dr. Vrushali Saraswat, a renowned happiness coach and gentle guide. In an age entangled by relentless pursuits, sharpened by cut-throat competition, and shadowed by the weight of material excess, life's tides often toss the heart into restless waters. Amid the whirlwind of demands and disquiet, true serenity becomes a rare and distant shore. This work arrives like a breath of stillness - timely, tender, and profoundly needed.

Spanning nine exquisitely woven chapters, this slender volume of just fifty pages unfolds like a quiet symphony of wisdom, each note resonating with the essence of true happiness and offering a progressive exploration of the fundamentals on which the edifice of happiness is built.

Dr. Vrushali Saraswat reminds us that ***"happiness is not a luxury; it's a necessity" - "not simply a fleeting emotion, but the fertile ground from which success, balance and fulfilment grow".***

Each page in the book brims with depth and practical ideas. Its pages radiate clarity, compassion, and practical insight, offering readers not just understanding but a roadmap for introspection. Through a graceful blend of timeless principles and pragmatic pathways, the work addresses the intricate dance of thoughts, emotions, and behavioural patterns, guiding the reader gently inward.

Chapter 7, "Lessons I Learnt from Curious Baby Groot," blossoms with wonder and quiet wisdom. Through tender case illustrations, the author stirs a gentle curiosity, nudging the reader to glimpse the hidden potential nestled within every soul.

It is a call to awaken - to gather one's scattered energies, to harness inner resources, and to walk the path of purpose.

The success stories shared do more than inspire; they plant seeds of possibility in the heart, leaving behind echoes of courage and a quiet determination to rise.

By weaving together the precision of science and the grace of soulful living, this work offers a harmonious tapestry - gently guiding readers toward lasting inner peace and happiness. It invites one to dwell in a continual state of mental upliftment, where clarity, contentment, and tranquility become enduring companions.

A mighty message this book offers: "You, too, can bloom".

Dr Ajit Kulkarni

M.D. (Hom.)

❖ ❖ ❖

ENDORSEMENTS

What if happiness wasn't something you chased, but something you trained for? In this life-changing 12-week journey, Vrushali blends science and soul to help you unlock lasting joy, from the inside out.

Ankur Warikoo,

Author

Uplift is a practical guide to mastering the inner game of happiness and success. Dr. Vrushali offers a rare blend of wisdom and action that creates lasting transformation."

Dr. C. H. Asrani,

Founder, Inches Academy

HEAR IT FROM THEM

"Uplift" is a very thoughtfully curated programme that connects all the dots from the present to the past and ultimately helps one understand the root causes of the patterns that hinder our growth and remove them from the core.

Thanks, Dr. Vrushali. For me, it was truly uplifting, as I could understand my limitations.

~Anuj Singhal

Delhi

❖ ❖ ❖

"Uplift" well, the name says it all! This journey of self-discovery unfolds layer by layer, much like peeling an onion—except with fewer tears and more 'aha' moments. Each session gently (or sometimes not-so-gently) nudges you inward, making you realize, Oh, so that's what needed to change!

The secret sauce of this program? Consistency and transparency. Dr. Coach masterfully guides you through self-reflection—sometimes with a pat on the back, sometimes with a well-placed push—but always with purpose. Change doesn't happen overnight, but as you go deeper, the bigger picture starts to come into focus.

I am incredibly grateful to ma'am for helping me recognize the hidden roadblocks I hadn't even noticed were holding me back. This experience has been nothing short of transformative, and I look forward to continuing these practices every day to stay empowered.

Thank you for making self-discovery feel so effortless—and even a little fun!

~Niki

❖ ❖ ❖

We humans are always in search of happiness, doing everything within our material capacity to find it. And when that search exhausts us, we realise that happiness was always within us. Laut ke buddhu ghar ko aaye.!

Dr. Vrushali helps the buddhu in us to find that happiness. She has built her own systems and step-by-step processes to reach what we are truly seeking. I really love how much research she has done to create these time-tested strategies that are making the journey easier for her clients.

Her program and content are truly useful for everyone and the warmth that Dr. Vrushali exudes makes the journey even more memorable.

Thank you,

~Nidhi Saini

❖ ❖ ❖

Dr. Vrushali is an amazing trainer on the power of the mind, gratitude, and manifestation. Her storytelling skills make the training interesting and easy to understand.

~Abhinav Thakur

It has been an extremely holistic healing journey. I have felt a major improvement in just two months. The ambience of the clinic is light and warm, and the counselling sessions are incredibly comfortable. Talking about myself has never been easy, but here, it was all made possible.

Thank you so much for helping me love myself again.

~Anaiya Dcosta

❖ ❖ ❖

Had a great experience at the clinic. Dr. Vrushali is a very skilled doctor and counsellor. She is a great listener and spends a good amount of time with each patient. I would definitely recommend going to her.

~Tejasvin Samarth

Chapter 1

Happiness: The Missing Link to Fulfilment and Success!

I am Dr. Vrushali Saraswat, and I have assisted individuals for more than two decades in managing their happiness and well-being. My work has always been motivated by a simple but profound truth:

Happiness is not a luxury; it is a necessity.

I am a *doctor by profession and a healer by choice.*

Over the years, I have worked with thousands of individuals from all walks of life, including entrepreneurs, business leaders, and professionals, and I have seen firsthand how happiness directly impacts success, productivity, and personal fulfilment.

I have interacted extensively with professionals and business owners over the past few years, and one consistent pattern stood out to me.

Many of them are struggling not with a lack of talent or ambition, but with an identity gap.

There is the person they are now and the person they want to be, the identity they've created for themselves through their ambitions.

If left unchecked, this gap can cause stress, burnout, and a persistent sense of dissatisfaction.

I remember working with Mr. Gupta, a business owner who came to me feeling overwhelmed and lost in his own goals. He had high goals, but he couldn't focus on what really mattered because he was caught up in the day-to-day chaos of operations.

I asked him to make a small change instead of giving him a long list of options: every morning, I asked him to define his intention and focus for the day. This simple shift in perspective helped him streamline his operations in just three weeks. And that, my friends, was only a small portion of Uplift, my 12-week transformational program that has helped a lot of people find clarity, equilibrium, and a new sense of purpose.

Why Happiness Is More Important Than We Think

After working with people for over 24 years to help them live better, more meaningful lives, I have come to understand that happiness is the bottom line of everything.

In my vast counselling experience, I have seen many businessmen optimising on their business knowledge, their systems, processes, and even team happiness, **but what about their own happiness?**

They feel that once I grow in my business, or once I buy this car or that house, I will be happy, and to buy these material things, they start running behind the wheel just like a hamster. They keep postponing happiness as if it will derail them from their growth journey.

However, when I establish the role of happiness in their lives, and also when they start feeling that life's more meaningful and easier, achieving their set goals and manifestations becomes a cakewalk!

Here I would love to share the story of a North Indian entrepreneur, when he focused on raising his happiness, his business started seeing great growth. After 3 months of Uplift, his revenue increased by 35%, and he stopped his high BP medication; his relationship with family improved, and his team alignment went up multifold, which reduced his stress further.

Every element of life, including relationships, profession, health, and general well-being, can not be balanced when happiness is deranged. We spend years searching for materialistic accomplishment, yet the inner fulfilment, a state of completeness, a state of enoughness, a state which we need, is never found outside or in material things.

As a result, I have decided to devote my life to researching, teaching, and creating happiness-based solutions that are not merely theoretical but also really useful and outcome-driven.

> Happiness is more than just a feeling, an emotion, or a chance event.
>
> **It is a shift in mindset, viewpoint, a science, and a practice.**
>
> Moreover, Happiness is just being **SAHAJ,** a state of ease in life, which, in reality, is not rocket science. It's just a feeling of being at ease with oneself and others.

It is something that can be cultivated, nurtured, and sustained, provided we are willing to make the right mindset shifts and lifestyle changes, through positive psychology, gratitude-based practices, and cognitive restructuring. All of these activities are a beautiful coherence of Western sciences with Eastern Philosophies. To add to all the concepts, I use various practical tools to enhance happiness.

I have helped over 27,000 individuals achieve lasting happiness and personal breakthroughs. My Happiness Index serves as a tool to measure happiness in a structured way, allowing people to track their emotional and mental well-being. The Joy Spectrum helps one define their life status, identify their problems and assets, and helps individuals optimise their lives.

Over the years, my work has led me to conduct workshops, seminars, and research on the science of happiness at both national and international platforms, including the AYUSH International Conferences in Dubai. I have been privileged to receive prestigious accolades, such as the International

Inspirational Woman Award and the Indian Health Professional Award, recognising my contributions to holistic health and happiness coaching.

My book Uplift, 12 Weeks to a Happier, Brighter YOU... is a culmination of everything I have learned, practised, and taught in my journey as a Holistic Happiness Coach, International Speaker, and Teacher.

It is a structured roadmap designed to help people bridge the gap between where they are and where they want to be, not just externally in their careers and achievements but internally, in their sense of fulfilment and emotional well-being.

I have strived to find solutions for people over the years, and that struggle has made me passionate about this work. I know what works and what doesn't.

My approach is not about temporary motivation or surface-level positivity; it is about creating deep, lasting transformation through scientifically backed practices that are easy to implement but powerful in their impact.

Why This Book? Why Now?

One of the most common questions I get is: If happiness is so valuable, why are you putting your knowledge in a book instead of keeping it as a premium service? The answer is simple: there are no free lunches in life, but there is always access to wisdom for those who seek it.

I truly believe that happiness should not be restricted to a privileged few who can afford private coaching or high-ticket programs. While personalised guidance has its place,

I wanted to create something that could reach more people, offering them real, actionable solutions to transform their lives, irrespective of where they are starting from.

This book is a summary of what I do and how I help people achieve their dreams by raising their Happiness Quotient. It is designed as a practical, step-by-step guide that takes you through twelve weeks of transformation, with each week focusing on a key aspect of happiness-building. You will find scientific insights, gratitude-based exercises, mindfulness techniques, and self-reflective prompts that will help you rewire your mindset, shift your emotional state, and create a life of joy and abundance.

Happiness is often misunderstood as something that comes after success, or after we gain a certain societal status, or acquire certain material symbols of wealth.

But the truth is that happiness is the foundation of success.

It is the driving force behind better decision-making, stronger relationships, increased productivity, and personal fulfilment, even longevity starts with Happiness.

If I wish for you to take one strong message home from this book, then it would be this:

"Happiness is easy, it's for everyone. Some are born with a natural ability to be happy; others just learn it through the walk of life".

❖ ❖ ❖

Chapter 2

Happiness is a One-Person Job

The happily ever after has poisoned our minds with a requirement that there's a prince charming who will come and complete our lives, and then we will be happy.

While here the reference is gender specific, the truth is that this construct and mindset are gender neutral. It's not just for girls, but it is true for boys as well, where the world becomes meaningful when he is able to fulfil certain requirements and meet specific standards set by society, and then only his existence will be complete.

This concept of another person or certain achievement completing us and making us whole is deeply flawed. It suggests that you require someone else to fulfil your happiness status, and your life will be complete only when you have someone else to care for or be cared by.

Happiness, however, comes from within.

Any external circumstances, relationships, or events do not influence it.

True happiness stems from inner awareness and self-reliance. In this chapter, we will look at how inner work and emotional independence allow people to cultivate a life of genuine joy despite difficulties in the outside world.

Through the story of Meera (Name changed for maintaining privacy of clients), a woman who faces the painful betrayal of her husband, we will understand the transformative power of taking ownership of one's happiness.

To emphasise my point, let me share the story of Meera,

Meera's Story: Betrayal and Rebirth

Meera was a 38-year-old woman with two children and a seemingly perfect marriage. Arjun, a man she utterly trusted, made her believe that she had found her life partner.

She devoted herself to her family for many years, putting their needs ahead of her own.

When she discovered Arjun's affair, her world crumbled.

The pain was overwhelming, and she felt like a victim of circumstances beyond her control.

The betrayal left Meera with questions:

- Why did this happen to me?
- Wasn't I sufficient?
- How do I move on?

Her happiness, once deeply intertwined with Arjun's actions and presence, was shattered.

She was first introduced to the concept of inner work and the realisation that happiness is ultimately a one-person job in the depths of this despair.

True Happiness is Founded on Inner Work Awareness.

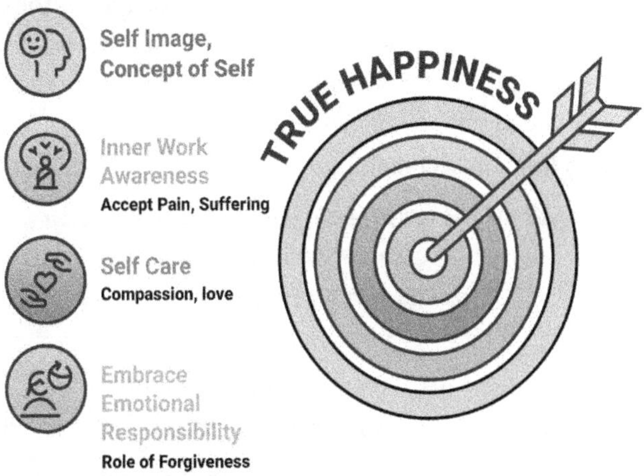

1. Recognising Inner Work

The conscious process of comprehending one's emotions, beliefs, and thought patterns is known as inner work. It necessitates turning inward, accepting pain, and transforming it into growth and self-awareness.

Meera began her journey with a simple yet profound practice: daily journaling.

She wrote about her emotions every morning without judging. She realised how strongly she had associated happiness with external validation, particularly from Arjun, through her reflections.

This was her first awakening:

My happiness was never mine; it depended on someone else. This thought process needed to be changed.

2. Embracing Emotional Responsibility

The next thing Meera did was accept emotional responsibility.

It wasn't about condoning the betrayal but understanding that her healing and happiness were her responsibility.

She started practising mindfulness and meditation, which helped her observe her thoughts without becoming consumed by them.

Meera discovered, through guided meditations on self-love and forgiveness, that there was strength in her pain.

As she acknowledged her emotions—hurt, anger, disappointment—she learned that these feelings were valid but did not define her.

The more she practiced, the more she reclaimed her power.

3. The Function of Self-Care

Without self-compassion, inner work is incomplete.

Meera treated herself with the kindness she would offer a friend.

She affirmed daily:

I am enough. I am complete. My responsibility is to make myself happy. This shift didn't erase the pain, but softened it.

Over time, Meera stopped looking for answers outside herself.

The betrayal was part of her story, but not the author of her happiness.

Not Relying on Others for Happiness: Breaking the Cycle of Dependency

1. The Fable of External Approval.

Many people, like Meera, believe that relationships, achievements, or external validation are prerequisites for happiness. Their sense of well-being, on the other hand, plummets when these external factors fail.

Meera realized she had given Arjun the power to control her emotional state.

Her happiness had hinged on his loyalty and actions. As she worked through this, she reclaimed that power.

The question shifted from Why did he do this to me?

to

How can I nurture my happiness regardless of what others do?

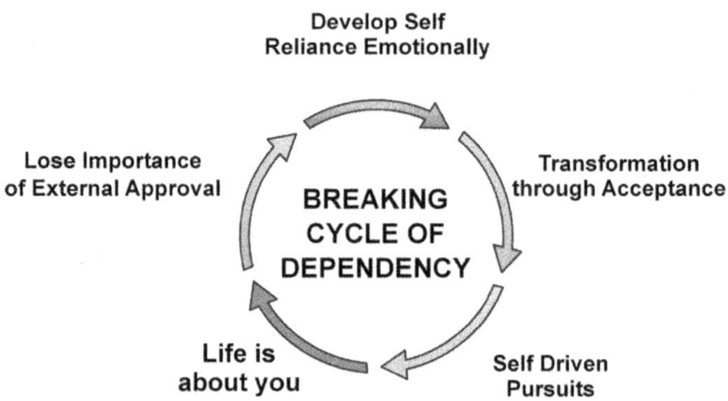

2. Developing Emotional Self-Reliance.

Emotional independence does not mean isolation.

It means finding joy and fulfilment from within while maintaining healthy, balanced relationships.

Nature walks, gratitude journaling, and hobby time were some of the rituals she created to reconnect with herself.

These practices anchored her happiness in her own actions and mindset.

3. Creating a Life That is All About You

Happiness flourishes when life is enriched with self-driven pursuits.

Meera discovered her passion for painting, a hobby she had set aside after marriage.

Each brushstroke became an act of self-expression and joy.

She felt a happiness that didn't depend on what other people did, as her days were filled with moments of mindfulness and creativity.

The Transformation: From Betrayal to Empowerment

A year after the betrayal, Meera stood in front of her canvas, painting a sunrise. The woman who once believed happiness was a shared responsibility now knew it was hers alone.

She was still navigating co-parenting with Arjun, so her circumstances had not changed, but her inner world had changed.

The profound truth revealed by Meera's story is that happiness is a one-person job. Breaking free of external dependence takes inner work, self-awareness, and courage.

The best part of this journey was, Arjun's focus came back on Meera, he repented his actions, and taking inspiration from Meera's commitment to self, he committed to the families' happiness.

So, the only change in equation one needs in a relationship is to be your own better version; everything else finds its own way to suit your requirements.

Practical Steps for Inner Work and Emotional Independence

1. **Daily Journaling:** Write about your emotions without judgment.
2. **Mindfulness practices:** include observing your thoughts for ten minutes each day.
3. **Gratitude for self:** Recite affirmations as though I am the one who makes me happy.
4. **Engage in activities:** that bring you joy to pursue your passions.
5. **Practice Gratitude:** List three things you are grateful for each day.

The journey to happiness starts within. It calls for the willingness to confront your inner world, the courage to let go of your dependence on others, and the determination to care for your own well-being.

Like Meera, anyone can reclaim their happiness when they recognise it as their sole responsibility. After all, happiness comes from within you, not from what happens to you.

❖ ❖ ❖

Chapter 3

I Knowitis

Knowledge is power only when you are applying it to your own life. In the current modern world of excessive connectedness and the social media boom of sharing the wisdom pearls by every Tom, Dick and Harry, "I know this," has become one of the most dreaded illnesses and therefore I love to call it as "I knowitis."

This has become one of the most common obstacles to personal growth.

People often mistake *familiarity* with *mastery,* assuming that mere awareness of a concept is equal to actually implementing it to the core.

However, knowing is just the first step; true transformation occurs only when knowledge is consistently applied.

chapter, we will debunk this myth and demonstrate how the UPLIFT program bridges the gap between knowing and doing. Upliftment is only achieved when genuine actions are taken towards personal growth.

I KNOWITIS

Why 'I Know This' is a Self-Sabotaging Belief

Uplift is a right-brain activation technique that helps you to release yourself from the deadly infection of this I knowitis. Once you break down what you know and figure out a plan as to what you will do with it, life becomes easy.

Uplift enhances your ability to take action on what you already know.

It's your gateway to implement and utilise the knowledge base and see the elevated results for yourself.

I knowitis is in reality 'self-sabotage', you can see it in this flow chart step by step.

I Knowitis
It's Familiar
Nothing New
Have Tried it
Do Nothing
Stay the Same
A New Concept
Practice Daily Application Steps
Break the Comfort Trap
Expose your Belief System
Break the Barriers of Repetitive Patterns
Have Daily Break Throughs
Tiny, Small Consistent Steps & Changes
Massive Results
Permanent Transformation
Lead a Happier, Fulfilled Life

Replace	By
I know Gratitude.	I express Gratitude for.
I have tried it before doesn't work.	I will follow the structure for 90 days & build momentum.
I don't have time.	I will make time for growth.
I can do this on my own	If I could have, I would have done it, let's follow a certain system.

Enough of dos and don'ts. Let me share a few real-life stories from my practice.

CASE STUDIES

From Knowing to Doing

Case Study 1

Maria Dela Cruz- The Gratitude Skeptic (Philippines)

Maria, a 35-year-old marketing executive, claimed she already knew the benefits of gratitude journaling.

However, when her stress levels peaked, she realized she wasn't applying her knowledge through UPLIFT.

Maria followed the 90-day journaling challenge.

The consistent practice helped her manage stress, improve relationships, and cultivate a genuinely positive outlook.

She said, 'I knew about gratitude, but this program showed me how to live it.'

Case Study 2

Rajesh Sharma – The Mindful Procrastinator (India)

Rajesh, a 42-year-old entrepreneur, was familiar with mindfulness but never practiced it consistently.

He often said, *'I know this,'* dismissing the need for guidance.

After joining *UPLIFT,* Rajesh committed to 10-minute daily meditations.

Within weeks, he noticed improved focus and better decision-making in his business.

He reflected:

'It wasn't the knowledge that changed my life;
it was the application.'

Case Study 3:

Anika Reyes – The Overwhelmed Mother (Philippines)

Anika, a mother of three, knew all about affirmations and self-care but rarely made time for herself.

The *UPLIFT* program's structured tasks gave her the push she needed to prioritize her well-being.

'I realized knowing isn't enough; doing makes the difference,' she said.

Today, she balances motherhood with self-care practices that uplift her mood and energy.

Case Study 4

Vivek Patel – The Corporate Achiever (India)

Vivek, a high-performing manager, thought happiness was a natural result of success. He understood the principles of positive psychology but remained stressed and unsatisfied.

UPLIFT introduced him to micro-moments of happiness, like practicing gratitude during breaks, shatpawali, and Magic Rock.

This simple practice transformed his daily experience.

'I knew the theory; UPLIFT helped me feel it,' Vivek shared.

Once you cultivate a sense of curiosity and start opening your mind with the intention of experiencing life, give them an opportunity to grow and expand their perspective.

The Implementation Advantage

UPLIFT is not about teaching you what you already know. It's about helping you apply that knowledge to experience tangible, lasting changes.

The myth of *"I know this"* dissolves when individuals witness their own growth through consistent practice.

I knowitis: (Noun) it's a form of infection which has a great grasp on the younger generation today, as they have knowledge in their pockets today, they can search for anything with a few clicks and get the knowledge due to which they end up feeling that:

Knowing = Doing

But through the application of microconcepts and micro-practices of Happiness, one can easily get rid of this dreadful infection of knowing all and understanding that :

Knowing ≠ Doing

Action = Doing.

Knowledge is a treasure, but practice is the key to it...

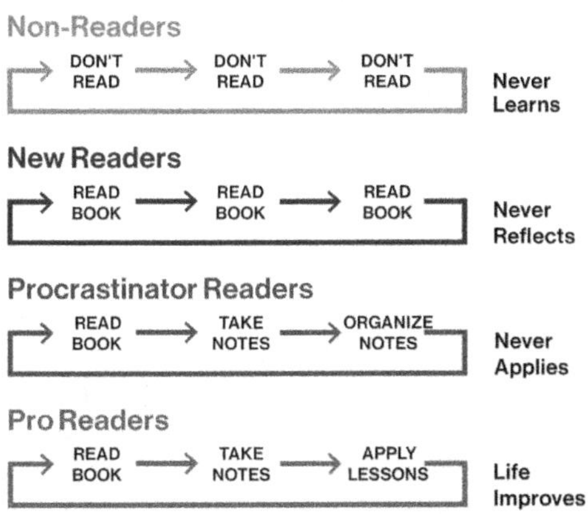

Just by knowing something, one doesn't become an expert. This can be very well explained by an example of book readers from the above diagram.

Non-readers never read, and therefore never learn anything, new readers read and don't reflect on it, procrastinators read, take notes but don't apply. Pro Readers are the ones who are the only ones free of I Knowitis as they read, take notes, organise and apply the learnings in a way that their life improves.

Now, in today's digital world, we will have to include AI learnings or even digital content in the place of reading, but the states will remain the same.

If one wants to cure their I knowitis, they have to take action.

ACTION REAPS RESULTS...

Chapter 4

Tiny Teachers, Giant Lessons What I learnt from Ants

One day, I was sitting under a tree and I noticed a trail of ants working relentlessly. I got curious about the ants & observed them closely, what I noticed and learned from the ants blew my mind. They're delightful and work choice creatures, so they and their inconspicuous nature gave me big life lessons and left a lasting impact on my style of helping people achieve their goals.

Ants are fascinating creatures.

Tiny in size yet monumental in discipline, they exemplify consistency, teamwork, and the power of small, daily actions. Watching ants can teach us profound lessons about life, especially when it comes to creating happiness through consistent habits.

In this chapter, we will explore how the principles of daily discipline, small yet purposeful actions, and consistency can transform one's emotional well-being.

We will discuss the importance of practices like daily journaling, emotion mapping, setting daily intentions, and maintaining focus. And through relatable case studies from the Philippines and India, we will see how these simple but consistent practices have brought about lasting happiness.

The Myth of Sporadic Effort

In today's fast-paced world, many believe that happiness or emotional well-being can be achieved through occasional big actions, like a vacation, a promotion, or a major life change. However, this approach often leads to fleeting satisfaction.

The real, lasting sense of happiness comes from small, consistent habits repeated daily.

People often express sentiments like:

- "I tried journaling for a few days, but it didn't work."
- "Meditation doesn't help me; I did it once last month."
- "I know I should set daily goals, but I forget."

This inconsistent approach mirrors the behaviour of someone expecting a tree to grow after watering it once a month. Ants, however, show us a different path.

They don't build their colonies in a day; they persist, working step-by-step, day after day.

The Ant-Like Discipline

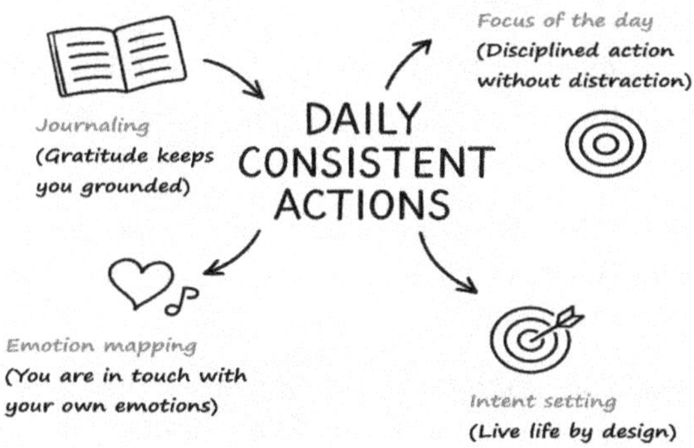

When one decides to solve this problem, they must look at ants for taking small actions consistently. Just as ants follow a pattern with unwavering discipline, we can build happiness through small, consistent actions.

The *UPLIFT* program incorporates a four-core practice, modelled after I understood why ants can build such huge anthills despite being so tiny.

1. Daily Journaling

- Journaling helps release emotional clutter and provides clarity.
- The act of writing daily creates self-awareness and reinforces positive thought patterns.

This reminds me of one of my patients, Angela, a 29-year-old high school teacher, who used to be emotionally drained and lacked self-care.

She did so much writing for her job that when I suggested she write for the Uplift program, she said it would not work.

However, she committed herself to a 12-minute journaling method each day, and within 10 days her frustration vanished.

She agreed pleasantly with me on the fact that when she applied discipline from Ants, her life improved to a great extent, and her burnout turned into a key self-motivated life mission to help children.

2. Emotion Mapping

- This practice involves identifying and understanding daily emotional states.
- By tracking emotions consistently, individuals can recognize triggers and patterns.

Let me share an example of why daily emotion mapping is a must.

In the fast-paced corporate or business life, intellect and logical thinking take the front seat, and emotions are, in reality, pushed aside.

This is what happened to Arjun, a 45-year-old Sr. VP of a multinational company.

He kept on losing on his performance, and also nearly started feeling that he was losing his business edge. He consulted many business coaches but couldn't succeed.

When he came to UPLIFT, he was actually on the verge of depression.

However, when he started mapping his emotions daily, he realised that it's anxiety of performance that is clogging his thinking. After regular emotion mapping, we found the pattern, and it was addressed in the RBA framework.

3. Daily Intent Setting

- Starting the day with a clear intent aligns thoughts, emotions, and actions

It helps participants remain focused on positive and growth-oriented tasks

A Delhi-based 2nd-generation businessman was struggling to set priorities in his work despite taking guidance from multiple coaches.

His actions were erratic and inconsistent.

Once he understood the power of scheduling his priorities and practiced a daily focused mannered learning, it brought big financial gains to this businessman.

4. The Focus of the Day

- This involves identifying the day's single most important task.
- It minimizes overwhelm and ensures purposeful, productive days.

The same businessman we talked about previously started doing deep intention + focus work.

Every day, once he sets his intention, he chooses one targeted area to focus on and run, thus, many tasks aligned and completed activities put his business in acceleration.

This discipline + focus is inspired by the definition, which was demonstrated -

"One stays on one thing until the job is done."

Benefits of Consistent Daily Practices

The discipline ants exhibit can transform our emotional landscape when applied to happiness practices.

Here are the key benefits of the UPLIFT approach:

1. **Greater Emotional Awareness:** Daily journaling and emotion mapping foster deeper self-awareness.

2. **Reduced Stress and Anxiety:** Knowing and tracking emotional triggers allows proactive management.

3. **Improved Focus and Productivity:** Setting a daily intent and focus streamlines decision-making.

4. **Enhanced Sense of Control:** Consistent practices instill a feeling of mastery over one's emotions and actions.

5. **Sustainable Happiness:** Small daily wins build momentum, creating a long-term foundation of happiness.

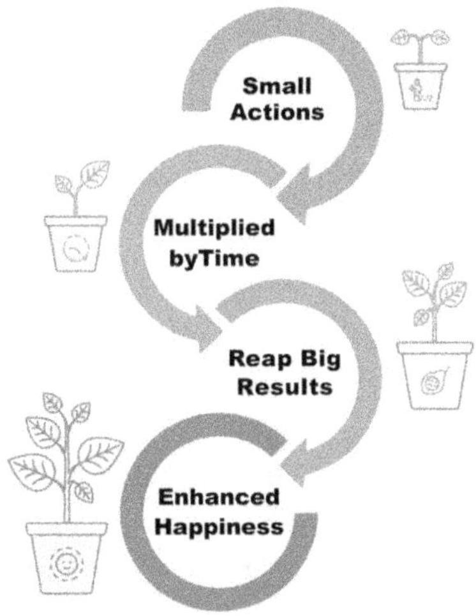

Ants may be tiny, but their wisdom in discipline and consistency is monumental. Like them, we can achieve emotional resilience and happiness by focusing on small, daily actions. The practices of journaling, emotion mapping, daily intent, and focused action provide a simple yet powerful pathway to well-being.

Just as ants build empires one grain at a time, we too can build our happiness one consistent day at a time.

❖ ❖ ❖

Chapter 5

The Power of Micro-Moments

Happiness is often perceived as a grand achievement—something to be attained after reaching significant milestones like career success, financial stability, or personal accomplishments.

However, true happiness is not found in a single event; rather, it is cultivated in the micro-moments of our daily lives.

Small moments of joy, connection, and mindfulness have the power to shape our emotional well-being. This chapter explores how embracing these micro-moments can create a profound impact on our overall happiness and fulfilment.

The Problem: Chasing Big Wins While Ignoring Small Joys

In today's fast-paced world, many individuals delay their happiness, believing it is tied to external achievements, making statements like:

- "I'll be happy when I get that promotion."
- "Once I lose weight, I will feel better about myself."
- "When I have more time, I will focus on my happiness."

These thoughts lead to a pattern of postponing joy, often resulting in chronic dissatisfaction.

The irony is that happiness does not come from one big event but from a collection of small, meaningful experiences.

The Solution: Recognising and Embracing Micro-Moments

Micro-moments are brief, intentional experiences that bring joy, gratitude, or connection. They may seem insignificant, but their cumulative effect can dramatically enhance overall well-being. UPLIFT incorporates these moments into daily life through simple, actionable strategies:

1. **Gratitude in the Small Things**

- Noticing and appreciating everyday moments, like a kind smile or a pleasant breeze.
- Counting your blessings for small things each day turns you into a much happier person.

2. **The Power of Presence**

- Fully engaging in daily activities, such as savouring your morning coffee or truly listening to a loved one.

- Mindfulness techniques help anchor attention to the present.

3. **Acts of Kindness**

- Small gestures, like complimenting someone or helping a colleague, create ripple effects of positivity.
- Making kindness a habit through intentional daily actions.

4. **Meaningful Connections**

- Take a few minutes to check in with family or friends.
- Sharing a moment of laughter or heartfelt conversation.

5. **Micro Self-Care Practices**

- Stretching for five minutes, breathing exercises, or journaling at night.
- Small, consistent acts of self-nurturing contribute to long-term well-being.
- Daily mood tracker, morning and evening.

6. **The Practice of Magic Rock:**

- Inspired by the book The Magic by Rhonda Byrne

CASE STUDIES
Transforming Lives Through Micro-Moments

Case Study 1

Miguel Santos – The Burned-Out Manager (Philippines)

Miguel, a corporate manager, was constantly stressed, waiting for his next big vacation to "finally relax."

Through *UPLIFT,* he began incorporating small mindfulness breaks into his daily routine.

By simply taking five minutes to enjoy his morning coffee without distractions, Miguel noticed a significant improvement in his daily stress levels.

He reflected, *"I used to think happiness required a big escape. Now, I see it in the smallest moments."*

Case Study 2

Priya Iyer – The Overwhelmed Mother (India)

Priya, a mother of two, felt consumed by daily responsibilities. She rarely had time for herself and postponed self-care.

Through *UPLIFT,* she started practising 12-minute Morning reflections and 8-minute evening reflections before bed.

Within weeks, she found herself feeling more centred and less overwhelmed.

Priya said, *"I used to think I needed a full day off to recharge. Now, I realise even small pauses can change my entire mood."*

Case Study 3

Arnel Cruz – The Socially Disconnected Engineer (Philippines)

Arnel, an introverted software engineer, struggled with social interactions. He often avoided conversations, believing they required long engagements.

Through *UPLIFT,* he started practising short, intentional connections—greeting colleagues sincerely and sending short messages to friends.

Over time, he built deeper relationships, saying,

"I never realised how powerful small conversations could be. They make me feel seen."

Case Study 4

Kavita Sharma – The Overachiever with No Time (India)

Kavita, a high-achieving entrepreneur, constantly postponed happiness for future goals.

After learning about micro-moments, she started integrating short gratitude reflections and spontaneous joyful activities, like dancing for five minutes when feeling stressed.

"I used to think happiness was in success, but now I see it in everyday moments," she shared.

Benefits of Embracing Micro-Moments

1. **Increased Mindfulness and Presence**

- Helps break the cycle of autopilot living.
- Enhances appreciation for everyday experiences.

2. **Reduced Stress and Anxiety**

- Small mindful pauses throughout the day prevent burnout.
- Engaging in tiny moments of joy elevates emotional resilience.

3. **Greater Emotional Connection**

- Strengthens relationships through small but meaningful interactions.

- Encourages authentic and heartfelt conversations.
- Listening improves.

4. Higher Overall Happiness Levels:

- Cultivates a continuous sense of fulfilment rather than delayed satisfaction.
- Reinforces the habit of noticing joy in everyday life.
- Better health, wealth, and relationships.

The pursuit of happiness doesn't require major life changes—it begins with small, everyday moments. Just as ants build empires grain by grain, we can build a life of happiness through intentional micro-moments.

Happiness is not a destination; it's in the pauses, the laughter, the gratitude, and the brief connections we experience daily.

Start today, embrace the small joys, and witness the profound impact they create over time.

❖ ❖ ❖

Chapter 6

Right Brain Activation Framework

Our brain, the human brain, is the wonder machine that has put all the researchers in awe and continuous work.

In spite of extensive scientific research work, we are not 100% sure as to how we think, feel, and act. Science can answer some questions, if not all. However, the 3-pound structure is our command center for existence.

It shapes our thoughts, emotions, feelings, actions, and in totality our experience of life.

The brain **is divided** into **2 hemispheres – right and left**

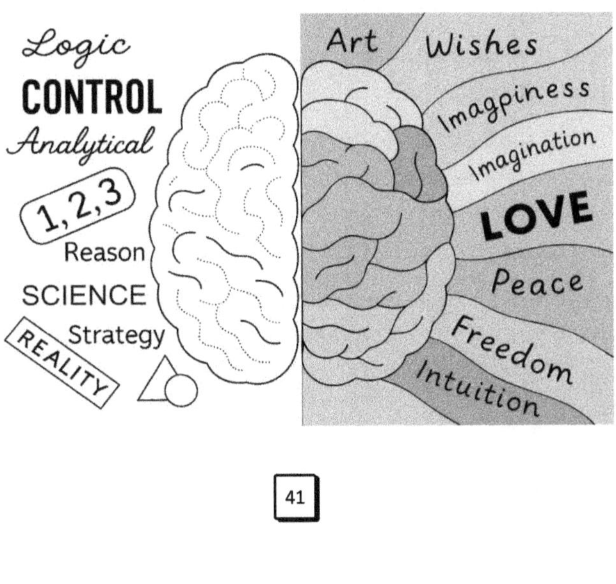

Left Hemisphere Functions

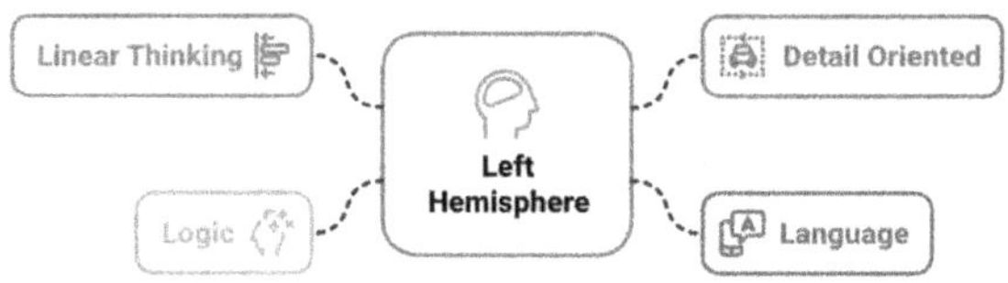

Right Hemisphere Functions

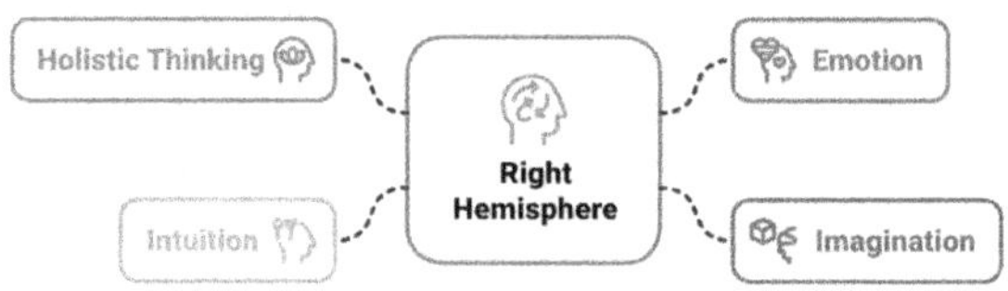

The right brain has an ability for abstract thinking, which perceives the bigger picture, embraces ambiguity, and enhances spontaneity with greater problem-solving capacity.

Now, one might think or question, how will embracing ambiguity help me?

Let me explain: It means that one is able to accept, and even welcome situations that are unclear, uncertain, or open to multiple interpretations, rather than seeking immediate certainty or clarity.

It involves an ability to be comfortable with the uncertain and an ability to recognise multiple perspectives and solutions possible for one circumstance.

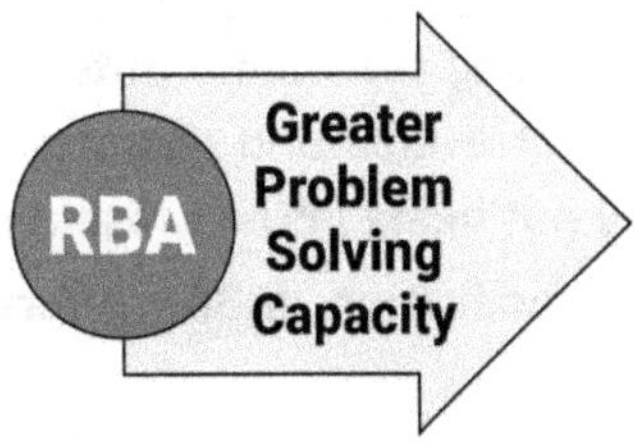

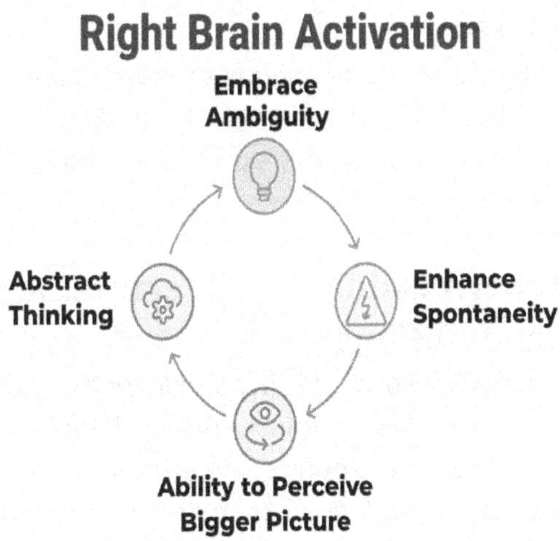

The fast pace of modern life has put most humans in the trap of an overthinking cycle, anxiety, and chronic stress.

The left brain thinking constantly puts an individual in the analysis of past events and distances oneself from savouring life by not being in the present moment!

The right brain activation (RBA) offers a powerful solution to this trap.

It creates a gateway to being present, connected, and emotionally resilient.

The RBA taps into the wellspring of creativity, intuition, and joy. With RBA, we are able to navigate through life's **challenges** with grace, equilibrium, balance, and equanimity.

The Modern Epidemic: Overthinking and Emotional Fatigue

- In today's world of hyper-connectedness, 24x7 overthinking and overanalysis have become robbers of joy. The most troublesome experience for today's youth is "being left on seen "; such a trivial act is capable of putting a teen in a state of self-doubt and self-sabotage.
- It is due to over-bombardment of our brain with information, demands, and expectations – there's no space for quiet contemplation and emotional rumination!
- Continuous state of analysis, evaluation, and fear-based expectation from the future – this left brain activity gives rise to chronic stress, emotional exhaustion, and a reduced capacity for joy, happiness.

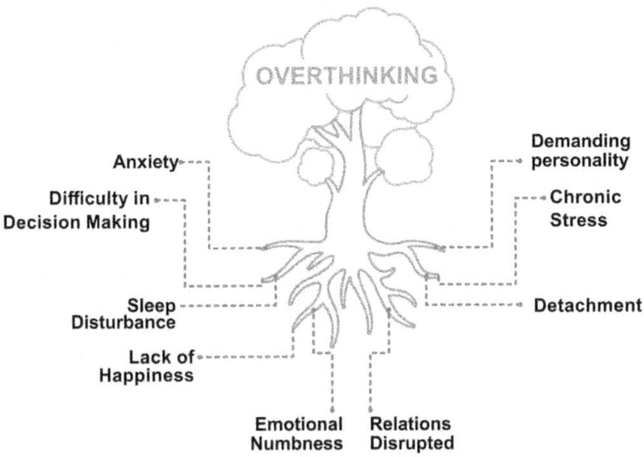

To disengage from this rut of overthinking best solution is to nurture and engage in RBA, which provides a better and fulfilling experience of life.

THE RBA Technique

RBA is an age-old science that empowers the individual to engage in creatively structured, holistic thinking.

1. Expressive Writing

Expressive writing is a powerful tool for stimulating the right brain, as it activates the shedding of emotional baggage. Whenever you speak, words flow out without much effort, but when you put pen to paper, words require a certain effort.

Aman, a Sr. VP of a multinational company, cured his insomnia simply by writing down his negative self-talk!

There are various forms of writing, and Uplift journal incorporates more than 10 forms, which ensures RBA through daily writing prompts.

2. Colouring and Artistic Expression

Art is a great RBA tool as it engages the right brain through visual, spatial, and motor skills. The eye-hand coordination required for artistic activities provides a great solution for digital detox, excessive rationalisation, and also allows us to tap into a state of flow where we can find our own self without the weight of judgement or restriction.

UPLIFT uses various art forms like colouring intuitively, zentangle, doodling, crochet, knitting, embroidery, sculpting, etc

3. Visualisation

Visualisation is a powerful tool that engages RB in creating a mental image of the desired outcome. Many successful people have documented evidence wherein they visualised a certain outcome and materialised it.

The most important benefit of visualisation is that it enhances optimism, clarity, and emotional regulation, relieving an individual from the epidemic of negative self-talk and chronic stress. Visualisation also paves the way for positive future progression.

4. Music and Dance

Music has the ability to change moods instantly with its vibration. The frequency of music has the capacity to resonate with brain waves. So when we play high-frequency music, one can transport oneself to the desired higher brain waves and can easily enhance one's problem-solving capacity as music directly activates the RB.

Dance is a physical activity, and any physical activity is capable of bringing about chemical changes in the body. Dance helps in the release of happy hormones, and hence, RBA is a great tool for happiness.

Rhythm in general fosters joy, connection, and a sense of aliveness.

Key Benefits of RBA

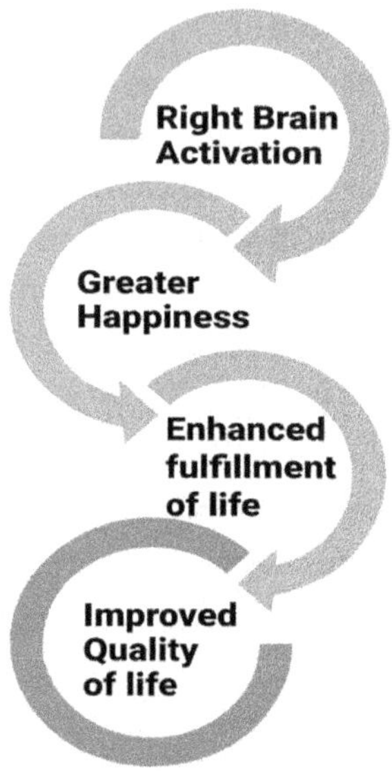

RBA tech is a transformative approach to cultivating lasting happiness and well-being.

RBA activation methods are scientifically proven techniques that cultivate joy, mindfulness, resilience, and a deeper connection to ourselves and empower us to see the world in an unconditional, nurturing manner, thus improving our relationship to self and others.

One can generate abundance, emotional equilibrium, and authentic happiness through the RBA techniques!

❖ ❖ ❖

Chapter 7

Wisdom of the Young Explorer

Curiosity is the mother of many innovations, findings, and discoveries in this universe. Similarly, curiosity is the engine of this lifelong train of our personal growth. Lifelong learning, transformation, and deep happiness emerge from our persistent state of curiosity.

Children tend to learn a great deal in childhood, but the same children, when they grow up, lose the ability to learn. The reason is simple

As children, we are curious, but as life grows on us, we dissociate from the curiosity, and that takes us away from our happiness.

To add to this, societal pressures, expectations, routine life, and belief systems act like an extinguisher of our curiosity.

Instead of questioning and being open to receive things, we start to assume and learn to settle for less.

A curious mindset is not just about learning something new. It's a state of mind.

It's a state that fosters and encourages adaptability, openness, acceptance, and the continuum of personal growth.

When we look at life with curious eyes, we encourage our free thought process, engage in the present moment, fuel our excitement, and nurture resilience.

All of this culminates in deep satisfaction.

One of my most beloved fictional characters, who personifies the spirit of curiosity, is Baby Groot from the Guardians of the Galaxy franchise.

Groot doesn't speak much in the entire movie, but Groot's actions speak volumes. His eagerness to explore, his ability to adapt to a variety of different environments, and his unshakable ability of openness and acceptance of new experiences demonstrate the true nature of curiosity.

Just like Groot, embracing, accepting, and imbibing a true sense of curiosity is the doorway to continuous personal growth.

The Closed Mindset

Many people get into the trap of having a fixed mindset, in which they firmly adhere to their preconceived notions, avoid difficult talks, and refuse new experiences.

A closed mindset frequently leads to:

- Resistance to new ideas and perspectives
- Stagnation in personal and professional growth
- Increased stress and frustration when faced with unexpected challenges
- Missed opportunities for deeper relationships and insights
- Fear of change and uncertainty

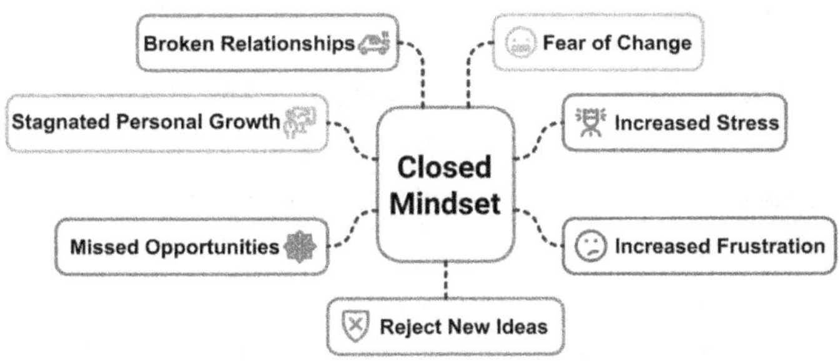

In contrast, personal freedom, creativity, and happiness can all be achieved with a curious mindset. A world of possibilities opens up to people who are willing to learn, flexible, and open to new experiences.

Living a Life Filled with Curiosity.

To develop a curious mindset, one must actively cultivate a sense of wonder, ask thoughtful questions, and remain open to learning from every experience.

The following are key advantages of embracing curiosity:

1. Enhanced Problem-Solving and Innovation

People are more likely to find solutions to problems that others might overlook when they are curious. When faced with a challenge, a curious individual will explore multiple possibilities rather than being stuck in a rigid approach.

Like Groot, who is constantly investigating his surroundings and finding unconventional solutions, adopting an exploratory mindset helps individuals tackle problems in unique ways.

James Cartwright (Name Changed) – The Stagnant Engineer (UK)

James, a 42-year-old mechanical engineer, struggled with career stagnation.

He avoided learning new skills because he believed that his prior knowledge was sufficient, and his work felt repetitive.

He was encouraged to approach problems with a beginner's mind at an innovation workshop. In one of the sessions of UPLIFT, his inner childish curiosity was stirred, and he started asking more questions from then on, investigating new technologies, and working with younger employees.

James led a ground-breaking project within a year that brought the production system of his company up to date.

James led a ground-breaking project within a year that brought the production system of his company up to date.

"Curiosity made me fall in love with learning again, and it completely revived my career," he remarked later.

2. Greater Adaptability and Emotional Resiliency

Curious individuals are better equipped to navigate uncertainty. Instead of fearing the unknown, they embrace change with enthusiasm, seeing it as an opportunity rather than a threat.

Despite his limited communication, Groot quickly adjusts to new challenges and never lets them stop him from exploring. He serves as a reminder that being flexible builds resilience.

Aditi Rao (Name Changed) – The Burned-Out Entrepreneur (India)

Aditi, an entrepreneur who is 36 years old, faced the prospect of her startup failing.

Initially devastated, she resisted the idea of starting over.

In one of the sessions of UPLIFT, she was introduced to asking lofty questions, and she embarked on an awakening from this session.

"What can I learn from this experience?"

She began exploring new industries, attending business conferences, and networking with different professionals.

This curiosity led her to an unexpected opportunity in digital marketing, where she found renewed success.

She shared, "Curiosity not only helped me move on; it helped me redefine my path."

3. Deeper Connections and Stronger Relationships

People's genuine interest in one another is stoked by curiosity, which in turn leads to deeper, more meaningful relationships. We listen more deeply and gain a better understanding of other points of view when we are curious about them. Like Groot, who builds relationships effortlessly despite communication barriers, a curious mindset helps individuals connect with others on a deeper level.

The Distant Father, Mateo Garcia, Philippines

Mateo, a 50-year-old businessman, had always struggled to connect with his teenage son, Rafael.

Conversations were minimal, and there was a growing emotional distance between them.

After the session about the power of curiosity in relationships, Mateo began asking Rafael open-ended questions about his interests.

Slowly, their bond deepened as Rafael felt truly heard.

"I realised I didn't need to 'fix' anything—I just needed to be curious and listen," Mateo said. His curiosity led to a newfound connection that transformed their relationship.

4. Increased Personal Growth and Lifelong Learning

Curious people never stop evolving. They continuously seek knowledge, embrace new skills, and expand their understanding of the world.

An open-minded person thrives by embracing lifelong learning, just as Groot eagerly explores new planets and adjusts to new environments.

Eleanor Adams – The Retired Teacher Who Kept Learning (UK)

Eleanor, a retired 67-year-old teacher, feared that retirement would make her life monotonous.

This fear landed her in depression.

While doing the UPLIFT program, she learnt the art of being curious in life, and she decided to nurture her curiosity by enrolling in online courses, exploring art, and joining a book club.

She made new friends, went to new places, and learned skills she never could have imagined thanks to her active participation in education.

She reflected, "Curiosity gave me a new sense of purpose and kept me young at heart."

5. More happiness and fulfillment

Curiosity transforms ordinary experiences into extraordinary ones. People discover wonder in everyday life when they remain open to discovery. The beauty of remaining curious can be seen in Groot's simple joy at exploring and interacting with his surroundings.

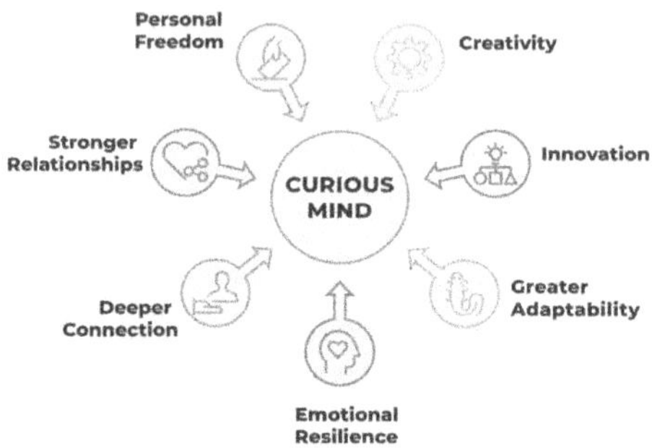

Curiosity is a potent tool that has the potential to alter our way of life. We can develop, adapt, and find joy in the unknown with a curious mindset. Curiosity keeps us open to new possibilities, whether in personal relationships, in advancing our careers, or in overcoming difficulties. Like Groot, when we embrace a sense of wonder and openness, we unlock a path to deeper happiness, resilience, and lifelong fulfillment.

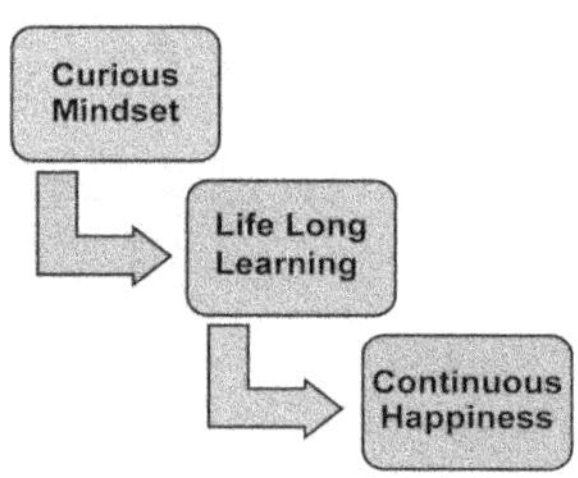

Armed with a 'Curious Mindset', instead of fearing change, we welcome it; instead of resisting new perspectives, we explore them.

Chapter 8

"Why We Do What We Do: Understanding Human Behaviour with T.F.C.A.R."

A human is always concerned about "What's in it for me?" Whatever we do, we are taking some lessons, learning, and understanding from the results we get. The result in one area usually defines our future in many areas of our lives. To get into details, let me share an example.

Rani Labels Herself Irresponsible

Rani loved dancing, she was just 6 years old when she was preparing for her annual program in school. She was playing music from the old-fashioned tape recorder. Her younger brother, who was 2 years old, came running into the room from outside, and his foot got stuck in the tape recorder wire. He stumbled and fell on his face. He got a huge cut on his chin and started bleeding profusely.

When their mother heard the commotion, she came running and, seeing her son with a wound and associating that it happened due to Rani's tape recorder, her mother impulsively slapped Rani for being a careless elder sister.

This incident got etched in Rani's mind. She concluded many things from this small incident.

The top conclusions were:

1. Her mother doesn't love her.
2. Second, my mother doesn't want me to dance.
3. Third, I am not responsible.

Rani stopped dancing. Now, all these feelings got suppressed or repressed as she grew up.

However, as a result of this incident, other emotions remained trapped in her mind.

Many years later, Rani had a son. When he was 8 months old, he fell down and cut his lip.

Rani panicked, and all those experiences of her childhood came back rushing to her.

She again felt that "I am not responsible enough."

This thought gave her anxiety, and she developed Panic disorder.

When we dug deeper into her panic, we identified these suppressed emotions and also identified her need for appreciation, her sensitivity to rejection, at the root of most of her actions in life.

Sameer: The Angry Young Man

Sameer, a successful entrepreneur, struggled with his anger management.

He would either shout or yell at his employees or relations, or he would stop communication with an expectation of them understanding.

When we explored, we found out that his father never engaged with him, and he felt deprived of love from his father, and as a child, he got angry.

Those same feelings are now projected out whenever anything unpleasant happens.

When one is determined to and works on, or seeks help in understanding these feelings or reasons for a certain pattern in our life, we can... All one needs to do is become aware and take action.

Thoughts

Thoughts are the logical left-brain thought process.

Thoughts are those that come up after proper analysis and evaluation of the pros or cons of any circumstance.

e.g.:

1. A person suffering from Diabetes choosing not to indulge in sugary food is a thought.
2. A financially broke person choosing to live frugally and save every penny wherever he can is a thought.

We can define thinking as the processing of experience, or gathering information, or rearranging information/ inputs from the environment, along with the information stored in our mind in the form of long-term memory.

We can say that thinking has its seat in the brain and is deeply influenced by past experiences, knowledge, emotions, and attitudes.

A thinking process is a chain of thoughts, often leading to a conclusion. It's either based on inductive or deductive logic.

***Ref: Foundations of Psychology & Homeopathy.**

Normal thinking has certain characteristics:

1. It must be aimed at a certain predetermined goal.
2. A normal thought is flexible.
3. It comes out of a strong purpose.
4. It is susceptible to motivation.
5. It doesn't get compromised by emotion.
6. It relies on logic: Inductive or deductive logic.
7. It doesn't rely on experiences of the past alone, it is capable of detaching from the emotional burden.

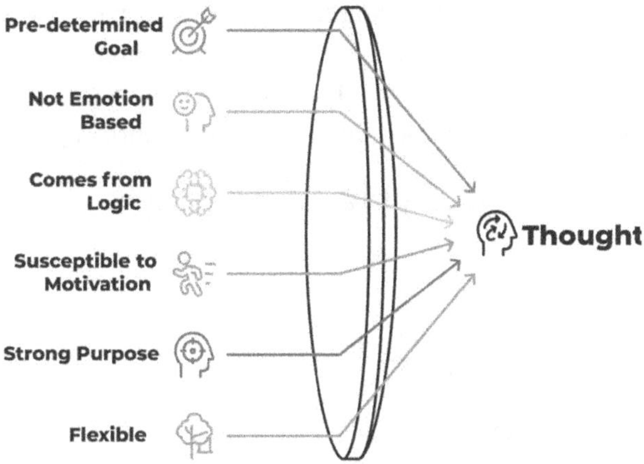

Feelings

Emotions, feelings, and moods are often the words that are used interchangeably, however, there is a lot of difference between the three..

Emotions are basic; a combination of what one knows and what one doesn't know about oneself.

In other words, emotions are a combination of conscious and subconscious phenomena.

To simplify, emotions are Energy in motion.

Feelings are always conscious; one is always aware of how one feels. Feelings are the gateway to our emotions we easily understand what one is going through when we explore the feeling state.

In the model of TFCAR **(Thoughts, Feelings, Conation Action and Results),** feelings give more equivocal evidence into the emotional patterns of the individual and can explain the "Why" of most of the actions and results a person gets.

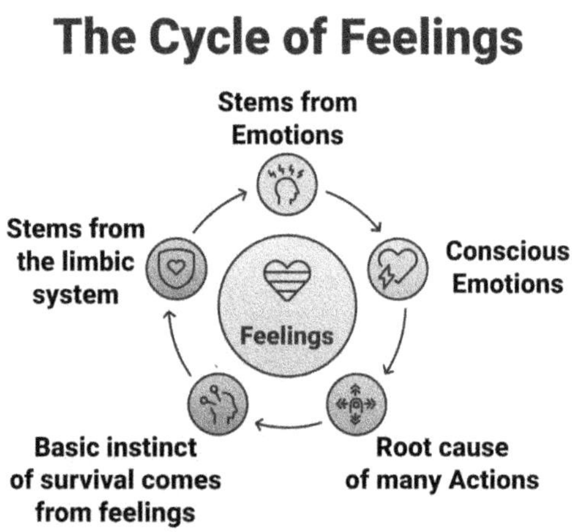

Conation

Conation is the scientific name for Behaviour.

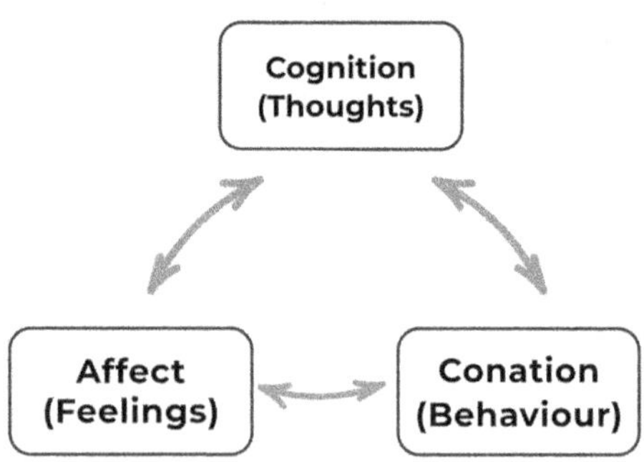

ACC is the famous triangle of human psychology.

Whatever we do is emerging out of this.

Conation/Behaviour is that part which gets trivialised as being superficial however, it is the external face of the human mind.

Behaviour is also carried forward through generations, it can also be an acquired quality for an individual.

Factors Influencing Human Behaviour

All these factors determine the Behaviour of a person.

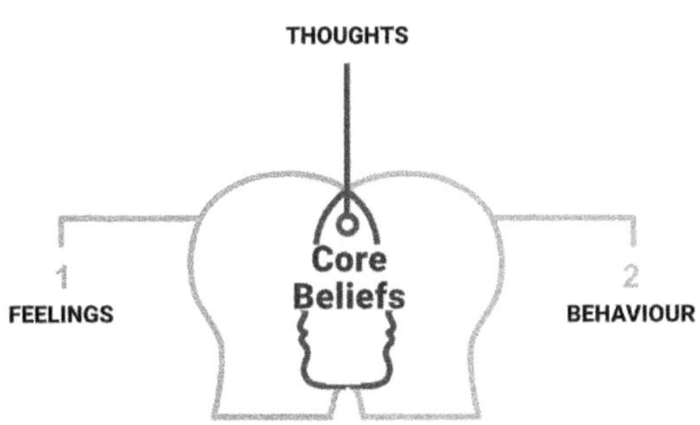

All these 3 factors, which are emerging from one's core beliefs, are responsible for the actions and results that one gets.

When we evaluate any incident in the grid of TFCAR, we are able to access a pattern of core beliefs of a person.

Once we understand the core beliefs, we can consciously remove the irrational pattern.

With the help of happiness tools, we can create new rational patterns that will uplift the person and raise their happiness quotient.

❖ ❖ ❖

Chapter 9

The Joy Spectrum – Mapping the Journey to Happiness

Happiness is not a singular, fixed state but a dynamic journey marked by growth, discovery, and deeper understanding.

To better navigate this journey, we introduce the concept of the *Joy Spectrum.*

This framework helps individuals identify their current relationship with happiness while providing a roadmap for growth. The spectrum consists of distinct stages that individuals pass through as they evolve in their understanding and experience of joy.

What is the Joy Spectrum?

The *Joy Spectrum* is a continuum that illustrates the progression from seeking happiness to becoming a source of joy for others.

It recognizes that happiness isn't merely about feeling good but about the conscious cultivation of inner well-being and external impact.

Each stage represents a shift in perspective and action, revealing how happiness evolves when nurtured with intention.

The spectrum acknowledges that joy is not an isolated occurrence but a series of transformative experiences.

As individuals move through the stages, they learn to harness gratitude, purpose, creativity, and connection to experience deeper fulfillment.

Key Features of the Joy Spectrum:

1. **Dynamic Progression:** The Joy Spectrum is not linear; it allows individuals to move forward or revisit earlier stages based on life experiences and reflections. Growth in happiness is often a spiral, with each revisit deepening understanding.
2. **Self-Awareness and Growth:** Each stage encourages introspection, helping individuals recognize their current patterns of joy and areas for growth. Self-awareness serves as the foundation for genuine happiness.

3. **Action-Oriented Framework:** Happiness requires action. The Joy Spectrum is built around actionable steps that help individuals consciously cultivate joy rather than passively waiting for it to appear.
4. **Balance of Internal and External Joy:** The spectrum highlights how internal shifts in mindset influence external experiences and relationships. True joy, as reflected in the spectrum, is deeply personal yet profoundly connected to others.
5. **Universal Yet Personal:** While the stages of the spectrum are universal, the experience of moving through them is unique for each person. Personal stories, practices, and reflections make the journey distinct.

The ***Joy Spectrum*** is based on the ***SPIRE Model of Happiness,*** wherein we evaluate or study happiness in Spiritual, Physical, Intellectual, Relational, and Emotional aspects in detail, hence it's the most holistic approach to Happiness evaluation.

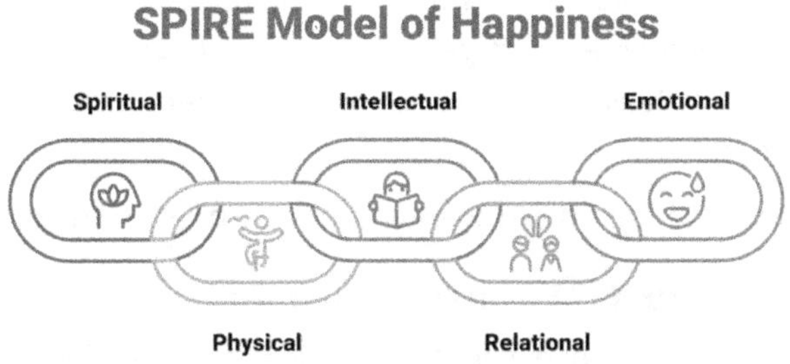

Stages of the Joy Spectrum:

The spectrum comprises five stages—Seeker, Creator, Innovator, Prodigy, and Luminary. While each stage will be explored in detail in subsequent chapters, here is a brief overview:

- **Seeker:** The initial stage where individuals are curious about happiness and actively search for it.
- **Creator:** The phase of experimenting with practices and crafting joyful moments.
- **Innovator:** A stage characterized by refining practices, introducing novel ways to experience joy.
- **Prodigy:** Marked by mastery of happiness techniques and sharing insights with others.
- **Luminary:** The pinnacle of the spectrum, where individuals embody and radiate happiness effortlessly, influencing entire communities.

The Joy Spectrum serves as both a map and a guide. It helps us understand where we are, recognize how far we've come, and envision the path ahead. By understanding the principles behind each stage, we can move beyond fleeting moments of pleasure to a life infused with deep, sustainable happiness.

Let's delve deeper into the exact meaning of each stage:

The Seeker (HI score below 45)

A score in this range suggests challenges in achieving a high sense of well-being and ambitious nature, but with a lower level of satisfaction, lack of positive emotions, or lack of clear purpose. Individuals here may be facing stress or dissatisfaction across various areas of life.

This range of scores suggests:

1. Very rare moments of joy or relief.
2. Infrequent moments of positive phases, however, in those moments, resilience is demonstrated.
3. Social connection is there, even if it is mostly strained.
4. There's a strong desire to improve their situation, hence, a seeker.
5. Frequently experience negative emotions or stress and require targeted emotional support.
6. You struggle to find purpose and could benefit from purpose-driven practices. Lack of clarity on your purpose is one of the main reasons for dissatisfaction with yourself, and hence, seeking out a source of clarity from outside.
7. Require relationships and strong support for feeling fulfilled. Loneliness is both a habit and a big challenge for you.
8. Experience challenges in work, personal life, and relationships due to overly emotional responses to not-so-overly emotional situations.
9. Often, they feel overwhelmed or fatigued and need a lot of validation from outside.

10. You require guided help to rebuild emotional strength and resilience.

Know where you are on the ***Joy Spectrum***

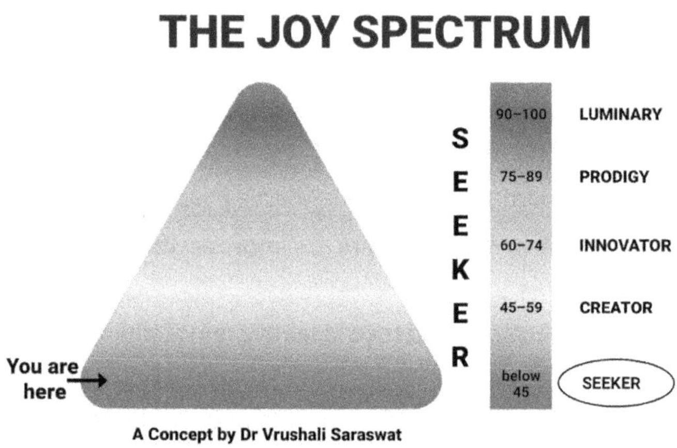

More About You

You are a seeker, meaning you are someone who's seeking things from the outside world and is in a dreamy state always. Your ambitions and reality have a huge gap.

This gap is easily bridgeable, however, your intentions and actions need a lot of guidance. You need a clear, simplified framework to get better results in life. You seek a lot of approval and validation from the relationships, this approval and validation or appreciation you need are based on your expectations, and these expectations are not conveyed to others hence, whatever others do that isn't enough for you, this is one of the main reasons of your dissatisfaction with others, these could be your spouse, best friends, parents or employees. You tend to get into a grumpy mood after an argument, and coming out of an argument with logic is difficult for you.

Seekers experience a great deal of challenges at the workplace, as they expect others to understand their needs, which leads to an emotional reaction to the professional setup or work. At times, simple tasks can appear as torture or trouble due to your emotional nature.

However, when someone explains the detailed logic behind their actions, you are easily persuaded to believe that the other person is not tormenting you. You have the ability to see another's perspective only when someone else explains it to you, but once you see another person's perspective, you demonstrate great friendship.

What Can You Do?

1. Identify your limiting beliefs and work on resolving your conflicts.
2. Train yourself to give logic-driven responses to situations rather than emotional responses.
3. Work on daily habits and mindset.
4. Take support from experts on how to effectively utilize the unlimited potential you have inside of you. Working closely with a Life/Happiness Coach can give you better perspectives with less effort.
5. To have better relationships, you must work on your concept of Self and love yourself.

Embracing your journey as a Seeker is the first step toward unlocking the happiness and fulfilment you deserve.

Remember, with the right guidance and intentional action, you have the power to transform your challenges into opportunities for growth and joy.

The Creator (Happiness Index Score between 45 - 59)

This score indicates low Happiness, moderate well-being, with room for growth in Happiness Quotient. People in this range may feel content at times, but may not consistently experience high levels of satisfaction or purpose.

This Range of scores indicates:

1. Fluctuating emotions with moments of positivity.
2. The feeling of occasional contentment indicates the potential for deeper satisfaction.
3. You are able to maintain relationships that provide you with some sort of support.
4. You show resilience only when faced with extreme challenges.
5. There's an innate tendency to give up.
6. You face challenges in balancing responsibilities that involve other people.
7. The stress impacts your mental as well as physical well-being.

8. You experience moments of doubt or low motivation that require continuous guided practices.
9. The low levels of Happiness impact confidence, which calls for a motivation boost.
10. Stress management is the biggest challenge, which impacts the best-made plans and becomes the biggest hurdle in the growth journey.

*Know where you are on the **Joy Spectrum***

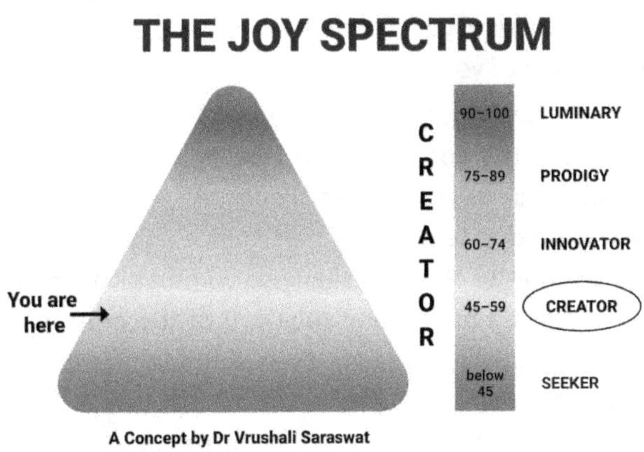

More About You...

You are a creator, meaning you are in that phase wherein you can create your destiny, however, you require external support.

You have acquired all the essential ingredients of success, but your own stress management is your challenge. All of this can be solved with simple and easy methods, which have been a secret of many ordinary people who rose to extraordinary success.

Creators are those who think that they work better under pressure and voluntarily avoid managing stress. They tend to nurture stress rather than good mental health. However, you have a great sense of purpose, and once given strong support, can move mountains.

Inconsistency in efforts is a hallmark of your personality; any small failure or misfortune, and you will easily decide to give up. In reality, you just need a little push, and you can achieve the life of your dreams.

You have incredible potential, which surfaces only when you are pushed to the corner. In the face of a challenge, you are capable of showing great resilience. All this potential is mostly wasted due to a lack of persistence and lack of self-confidence. Due to these challenges, communication with others becomes a hurdle and robs you of the opportunity to become an inspiring leader. Even when you attempt to lead your team or tribe, you face criticism due to a lack of persistence and effort, which in turn makes you more lethargic and demotivated.

With continuous support and guided motivational practices, you can optimise your hidden potential and embark on a remarkable success journey. Showing resilience is your secret superpower.

What Can You Do?

1. Stress management with Mindfulness practices and regular physical exercises.

2. Building consistency through scheduling minutely.
3. Building resilience and consistency through managing emotions by identifying emotional conflicts and resolving them.
4. Boosting confidence by implementing Self-love techniques, mindfulness, and gratitude.
5. Take support openly from a counsellor/life coach/ happiness coach for enhancing your life skills and optimizing your potential.

Remember, being a Creator means you hold the power to shape your destiny. With the right support, persistence, and guided practices, you can unlock your full potential and embark on a fulfilling journey toward lasting happiness and success.

Believe in yourself—you are capable of incredible things!

The Innovator (Moderate Happiness Happiness Index Score 60-74)

This range of scores indicates:

1. You experience mixed emotions, positive and negative.
2. You maintain a fair sense of fulfilment.
3. Have meaningful relationships, though sometimes inconsistent.

4. You are able to balance life and work, though not always smoothly.
5. You demonstrate signs of resilience but require support to maintain this.
6. You are able to engage in fulfilling activities, however lack consistency.
7. You exhibit moments of self-doubt that require attention.
8. Self-care practices are sporadic and need a structure to bind them.
9. You are able to identify and address growth areas; however lack of consistency makes you appear like a procrastinator.
10. You have all the ingredients to be your own light, but you require an outside structure or system that can lead you.

Know where you are on the ***Joy Spectrum***

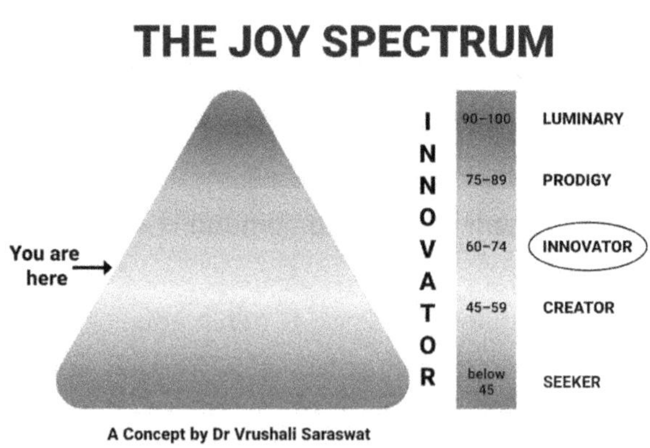

More About You

You are that unique combination that has all the ingredients for success, but hasn't put it together yet. All the aspects of your personality are great foundations for success, you can achieve whatever you decide on but one of the biggest hurdles is your lack of consistency and lack of persistence because of which you keep innovating new ideas, new products new methods of living life but don't give time to integrate what you have. There is a tendency to leave things halfway by presumptuous shortsightedness or inability to trust your own planning. Hence, your life might look like a person jumping from one task to another.

To take your life to the next level and basically to integrate what you need is engaging in deeply fulfilling and science-backed consistent action, which is both easy and effortless, as well as a no-brainer and not time-consuming. Basically, activities that take less time and are super easy to follow through with.

You have great ideas, a very good ability to plan, and considerable socially acceptable social skills, which can actually make you a great leader. Your personality is that of a charming person who is liked by most people, but your main challenge is inconsistency with yourself.

Innovators need new challenges every other day; hence, innovators, however, if you channel all your energies into one thing, you can succeed 70% more than trying newer methods or tasks.

You have more potential inside you than you give value to yourself. You are a people pleaser and have a charming effect on people; hence, other people are not your challenge. You are an emotional powerhouse; you can manage yourself as well as the people around you, but the only thing stopping you from being a leader is your inability to stay on one thing, which is your most troubled area of life.

What Can You Do?

1. Prioritize your tasks and dedicate your energy to completing one project or goal before moving to the next.
2. Create a daily routine or habit tracker to help you stay committed and accountable to your plans.
3. Believe in the strategies you've created; give them the time they need to produce results rather than abandoning them prematurely.
4. Incorporate quick and effective self-care activities, like a 5-minute gratitude exercise or a 10-minute walk, to maintain balance.
5. Use your social charm and innovative mindset to inspire collaboration and seek mentorship for structured guidance from a Life/Happiness Coach.

Your potential as an **Innovator** is limitless when paired with focus and persistence. By channeling your energy into meaningful, consistent actions, you can transform your innovative ideas into lasting achievements.

Embrace your power, trust your journey, and watch yourself rise as a confident and inspiring leader!

The Prodigy (Good happiness Happiness Index Score 75-89)

This range of scores reflects:

1. High level of satisfaction.
2. Balance in life.
3. Mostly experiencing positive emotions.
4. A few areas in life need enhancement.
5. Maintain meaningful relationships most of the time.
6. You are capable of identifying areas of growth.
7. Need external ideas to sustain happiness.
8. The sense of purpose is there, but lacks consistency.
9. Need resilience when faced with challenges.
10. The foundation of happiness is there, but it can be shaken easily by external stressors.

Know where you are on the Joy Spectrum

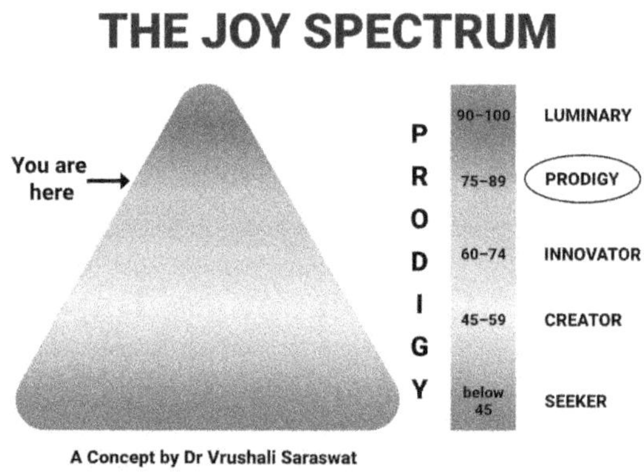

More About You

Your happiness score reflects a strong foundation and well-being in mind and body, however, you are prone to being swayed by external stressors.

You often experience a general sense of contentment with life. Most of your personal and professional achievements align with your values, giving you moments of pride and fulfillment. However, this satisfaction can sometimes be superficial, as it might not always translate into deeper happiness or a sense of purpose.

You have an inborn ability to bounce back from problems, however, you need direction and support. You strive to maintain harmony between your personal and professional responsibilities. While you do a good job juggling different aspects of life, there are times when stress or external factors disrupt this balance, leaving you feeling overwhelmed or stretched too thin.

Imagine how life will be when you don't need this external support and you become your own lighthouse. Can you imagine a life where problems come and go but don't affect your peace of mind? It is possible and has been practised by 100s of millionaires across the globe.

Your emotional state leans toward positivity. You feel joy, gratitude, and hope frequently, which provides a solid foundation for your well-being. However, negative emotions occasionally creep in, particularly when you encounter setbacks or face prolonged challenges.

You have a clear sense of what drives you and gives your life meaning. However, this purpose isn't always reflected in your daily actions, as inconsistency or distractions sometimes derail your focus.

What Can You Do?

1. Set specific, actionable goals for areas of improvement, such as relationships, health, or professional growth, and track your progress consistently.
2. Regularly expose yourself to new perspectives, books, or workshops that inspire you, and incorporate these insights into your daily life to sustain motivation.
3. Dedicate a fixed amount of time daily to align your actions with your sense of purpose, ensuring it becomes a habitual and integral part of your routine.

4. Seek professional help to further your determined goals and take structured guidance for future growth from a Life/Happiness Coach.
5. Make an effort to nurture your relationships by expressing gratitude, improving communication, and being present in your interactions.

Your happiness is built on a strong foundation, but the journey to thriving lies in consistency and resilience. By taking proactive, deliberate steps to address your growth areas, you can sustain your well-being and unlock deeper levels of joy and fulfillment.

Trust in your ability to create a balanced, meaningful life—you're closer than you think!

The Luminary (Highest Happiness Happiness Index Score between 90-100)

This range of scores indicates:

1. Exceptional well-being.
2. Highest level of satisfaction.
3. A strong sense of purpose.
4. Fulfilling social commitment.
5. Positive, optimistic person.
6. Engaged in a meaningful life.
7. Problem-solving expert
8. Impeccable health.

9. Clarity in decision-making.
10. Holistic leadership.

*Know where you are on the **Joy Spectrum***

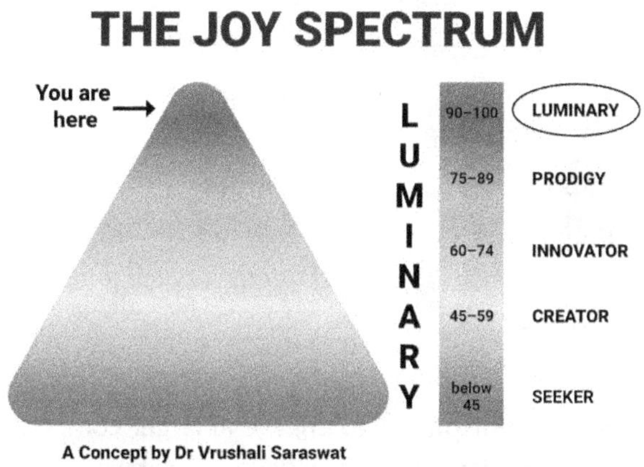

More About You

Your happiness index is a wonderful achievement, showing a deep sense of well-being and fulfillment. Continuous happiness at this level can lead to great success; consistently achieving this result is a game-changer for most successful people worldwide.

You radiate a sense of balance and harmony in every aspect of life. Your mental, emotional, and physical health align seamlessly, creating a life filled with vitality. Your critical thinking skills and calm demeanor allow you to tackle challenges efficiently, turning obstacles into opportunities.

Every action you take is intentional and aligned with your values, resulting in a fulfilling and enriched existence.

What Can You Do?

1. Mentor and Inspire Others

- Use your experience and wisdom to help others on their happiness journeys, becoming a beacon of positivity and guidance.

2. Strengthen Your Sense of Purpose

- Continuously evaluate and realign your goals to ensure they align with your evolving values and aspirations.

3. Expand Your Impact

- Seek opportunities to engage in larger community or global initiatives to amplify your positive influence.

4. Nurture Your Well-being

- Maintain your health and happiness through regular self-care practices like meditation, exercise, and gratitude journaling.

5. Continue Learning and Growing

- Commit to lifelong learning to keep evolving, both personally and professionally, while staying open to new perspectives.

As a **Luminary,** you embody the highest level of happiness and fulfillment, setting an inspiring example for those around you.

By continuing to lead with purpose and nurturing your well-being, you can create a ripple effect of positivity, making the world a brighter and happier place. Keep shining—you are a true beacon of joy!

Discover Where Your True Happiness Stands

You've just explored the Joy Spectrum. Now, it's time to go deeper.

What if a single step today could bring you powerful clarity about where you truly stand on your emotional well-being journey—and reveal your path toward a life of greater joy, balance, and meaning?

Introducing the Happiness Index

A transformational diagnostic tool based on the renowned SPIRE model of happiness, designed by Dr. Vrushali through decades of clinical insight and research into emotional and spiritual well-being.

This isn't just a quiz.

It's a mirror. A moment of truth.

And possibly, the beginning of a powerful personal transformation.

Chapter 10

Coming Full Circle: The Happiness Within

As we come to the final pages of this journey together, I want to take a quiet moment with you, the reader who made it to this point, who paused, reflected, and perhaps smiled at small awakenings along the way.

Uplift was never meant to be just a book. It is a living invitation, a twelve-week mirror held up to your soul, not to show you who you should become, but to remind you who you already are underneath the noise, the roles, the race.

Each chapter of this book was designed to gently peel away layers of old belief systems, of false expectations, of chasing happiness in all the wrong places. **And what lies beneath those layers is not a brand-new version of you,** but the real you. The one that had perhaps been buried under to-do lists, responsibilities, comparisons, and scars. The you that is capable of deep joy, wild resilience, and effortless contentment.

What You've Walked Through

You began with the understanding that happiness is not a reward for success; it is the starting point of it. You learned that it's not found in the distant future but cultivated daily through intention, presence, and self-accountability.

You examined how happiness is a one-person job that nobody else is responsible for, the garden of your inner life. You journeyed through the quiet wisdom of ants, the infectious curiosity of Baby Groot, and the practical power of micro-moments. You saw how right-brain activation through art, music, journaling, or dance can be a portal to self-healing. And perhaps most profoundly, you explored the T.F.C.A.R. model, how your thoughts lead to feelings, which create choices, actions, and ultimately, the results you live with.

And then, there was the Joy Spectrum. That powerful reminder that happiness is not a fixed destination, it's a fluid state, a rhythm we fall in and out of, as we grow, stumble, and rise again. Whether you're a Seeker, Creator, Innovator, Prodigy, or Luminary, you now have the tools to shift with awareness.

What This Book Isn't

This book doesn't promise a life without problems. It doesn't offer an escape from pain or a shortcut to perfection.

Instead, Uplift offers you the tools to walk through life, not around it. With a sense of grace. With a greater emotional vocabulary. With compassion for others, yes, but also for yourself.

It gives you structure without rigidity, discipline without shame, and accountability without pressure. It is not an attempt to change who you are but to reconnect you with who you've always been, before the world told you otherwise.

The Real Transformation

People often think transformation is loud. Dramatic. Obvious.

But the real transformation is often quiet.

It is the moment you pause before reacting.

It is the morning you wake up and feel less anxious, for no reason at all.

It is when you forgive someone not because they changed, but because you have.

It's when you look in the mirror and stop waiting for permission to love what you see. It is when your inner voice shifts from "I have to do this" to "I choose to do this."

These are the signs that UPLIFT is working its magic. Not externally, but internally, subtly, deeply, and lastingly.

Where Do You Go From Here?

This is not the end of your journey. It's the beginning of your conscious participation in it.

You now have a toolkit you can return to, whether you're facing burnout, relationship struggles, self-doubt, or simply an emotional rut. The gratitude journal. The emotion map. The micro-moments. The intention-setting practice. They are all your companions now.

Revisit the chapters. Repeat the 12-week process every year if needed. Make it your emotional annual audit. Let it evolve with you.

And remember:

Healing is not linear.

Growth is not always measurable.

You are allowed to bloom in seasons and rest in between.

A Personal Word from Me

As someone who has walked beside more than 27,000 people in their healing journeys as a doctor, a coach, and a human, I have learned this: no one is broken. Some are just weary. Some are just misaligned. Some are just waiting for a gentle nudge to remember their light.

You don't have to become someone new to be happy. You just have to stop betraying who you already are.

And if you've made it to this final chapter, I want you to know this:

You are more ready than you think.

You are more whole than you feel.

And your happiness is not far, it is just one conscious choice away.

Keep Spreading the Light

If this book brought value to your life, pass it on. Share it with a friend, a partner, a colleague, or a teenager finding their way. Start a journal circle. Host a 12-week Uplift group. Let this ripple outward.

Because when one person lifts themselves, they unconsciously lift others too. That's the real essence of Uplift: it begins with you, but it never ends with you.

Closing Intention

Let this final affirmation be your guide as you step into the world anew: **"I am enough. I am whole. I am capable of joy, even amidst chaos. And every day, I choose to rise gently, steadily, joyfully."**

Go ahead, go live your *Uplifted* life.

The world needs your light.

With love and belief,

Dr. Vrushali Saraswat

Happiness Coach, Healer, and Your Fellow Traveller

THE HAPPINESS INDEX

Why Take the Happiness Index?

- **Gain Clarity:** Understand how emotionally aligned and fulfilled you truly are.
- **Spot the Imbalances:** Uncover hidden areas that may be silently holding you back.
- **Receive Personalized Insights:** Get a custom happiness score and recommendations delivered straight to your inbox.
- **Start Your UPLIFT Journey:** Approach your personal growth from a place of understanding, not confusion.

Take the First Step

Scan the QR code and answer a few thoughtful, soul-stirring questions.

This process draws from Dr. Vrushali's 24+ years of experience supporting thousands in elevating their inner lives.

Important: Double-check your email and mobile number to ensure you receive your customized report.

UPLIFT Yourself

From where you are—

To who you were truly meant to be.

This is not just a test.

It's your invitation to awaken, align, and act.

Because happiness isn't something we find—it's something we create.

One choice at a time.

Start here. Start now.

Scan the code.

UPLIFT your life.

(Happiness Index.)

❖ ❖ ❖

www.ingramcontent.com/pod-product-compliance
Lightning Source LLC
Chambersburg PA
CBHW071352230926
51846CB00002B/527

* 9 7 8 9 3 6 3 3 8 4 7 6 7 *